Inspirations
from
the
Heart

A book of poetry, messages and humor!

Inspirations
from
the
Heart

A book of poetry, messages and humor!

by

Tory Griffin

Copyright © 2005 by Tory Griffin

Published by:
Voices Books & Publishing
P.O. Box 3007
Bridgeton, MO 63044
www.voicesbooks.homestead.com

Printed in the United States of America

Library of Congress Catalog Card No.: Pending

ISBN: 0-9770635-8-5

Dedication

This book is dedicated to the only true and living God who is the head of my life! Also to my mother Tunderleauh Griffin who has held on through trials and turmoil, and to those who need a word of healing and inspiration!

Acknowledgments

I appreciate all those who has been there on my side through thick and thin, who has encouraged me when I was down, who has prayed for me with great fervency and who has loved me for who I am; you know who you are! Thank you!

Tory Griffin

Preface

You never know what can be birthed out of a person when they are going through trials and tribulations. Maybe a song, poem or even a wise saying. What ever it may be, it is due to the circumstances they're facing or may have faced. The Bible tells us that trials make us strong, and we are able to comfort those that may face trouble due to the Lord delivering us from trouble. This book was inspired by God. It was through many circumstances I've faced, and is still facing, that I was able to write this book. While you read this book, you are reading my life story. Be encouraged!

So I

As the sun rises in the morning, so I wake.
As the sun lowers at night, so I lye
As my body thirst for water, so I drink
As my body decides to go to and fro, so I walk
As life's circumstances try to get the best of me, so I rise
As depression tries to imprison me, so I sing
As everything tries to shake me up, so I give thanks for that is the
will of God in Christ Jesus concerning me!

He's right there

I've been up and I've been down and almost leveled to the ground, but every time I turn around he's right there, I've been happy and I've been sad, there were many times that I was mad, Jesus Christ then made me glad, I know he's right there. My friends turned their backs on me they left me on my own, but God has never done me wrong, he's always there. Wherever you have been and wherever you are, Jesus Christ isn't far, he wants to heal your wounds and scars, cause he's right there.

I Am He

Up and down I go about the road of despair, I met a stranger along away, and he told me that he cares. I told him "I don't know you", but he replied, "but I know you". I asked him how?, he then showed me his hands and his feet and said, "see these scars?, they carry the sins of everyone including you!". I told him he reminded me of someone in the Bible who died for the sins of the world, he replied, "I am he".

· ı · ı · ı · ı · ı · ı · ı · ı · ı · ı · ı · ı · ı · ı · ı · ı ·

Stand Still

There was a man standing on an island that was the size of a floor tile. All he could do was stand still and hope that something or someone would come to his aid. As many hours and even days passed by, a helicopter spotted him and brought him out of his distress. The man told the pilot, "whew! you came right in the nick of time, for my legs were about to give in and I would've sunk in a water". Sounds familiar? Many times we go through trials and tribulations and it seems like we're on a small island. We can't move to the left or the right in fear that we'll fall. All we can do is extend our hands to balance our bodies (To extend our hands is to praise God because praise keeps us balanced!) and stand still and hold on to the hope that God has given us to wait on his deliverance. Time will pass and right before you are about to give up, Jesus will bring you out. In addition, the Bible tells us that the Lord keeps our bones strong, in other words, he keeps us standing. Like the song says, he may not come when you want him, but he's right on time! It may feel uncomfortable, but God wont allow you to completely sink and drown in the water. He comes right in the nick of time!

Wait

As my world get dimmer and my feet begins to shake, a still small voice reminds me to wait. As my patience shrinks and my soul begins to faint, that still small voice reminds me that I must wait. "Lord I can't take this anymore, you're really twisting my fate", but guess what I was told? you know, to wait. But as time goes by, I notice that I'm receiving strength. I can run further and never get tired. I can even fly. Then that still small voice came to me and said "But they that wait upon the Lord, shall renew their strength, they shall mount up with wings as eagles, they shall run and not be weary, and walk and not faint." I realize that I must wait!

I Need You

Every boat needs and nile
a girl needs a doll
a shovel needs a pile
and I need you!

Every duck needs a quack
a wolf needs a pack
a lunch needs a sack
and I need you!

Every bike needs a wheel
a fish needs a gill
the wounded needs to heal
and I need you!

Every girl needs a dress
a bird needs a nest
the weary needs some rest
and Jesus, I need you!

Make a Choice

There was a woman who was locked in a very small and dark room. She quickly panicked for she was claustrophobic. As time went by, the panic increased. She then stopped herself and said "Wait a minute, there is nothing I can really do right now to escape, so I have two choices either panic or calm down". So she sang a song. She sang and sang till someone outside heard it. The person was so moved by her beautiful voice that he busted the door open to see what was going on and the lady escaped out of the room. It's amazing how when the saints rejoice in their trials that the people around them get inspired! David said "my soul shall make her boasts in the Lord and the humble shall hear thereof and be glad, oh magnify the Lord with me and let us exalt his name together". Once you get them glad, next thing you know, they're rejoicing with you. Whenever you are going through a trial, instead of being discouraged and bitter, consider all the people you can reach and inspire through your worship! The world has too many problems of their own and when they see that you still have joy in the midst of yours, they would desire the Jesus in YOU!

Old School Testimony

Praise the Lord! Praise the Lord! I want to thank and praise God who is the head of my life. He's brought me from a mighty long way. I've been running for Jesus a mighty long time and I ain't got tired yet. He's my lawyer in the coat (court) room, a doctor in a sick room and a bridge over troubled waters. He's my bread when I'm hungry, water when I'm thirsty, a mother for the motherless, a father for the fatherless, a friend for the friendless and a shelter in the time of the storm. God is my all in all, he's everything to me. Healed me when I was sick, clothed me when I was naked, my lights are still on, heh! (praise break) pray my strength in the Lord!

Wait for your mate

I want what God has for me, I'll take nothing less, for when God gives it to me, it's always the best. So however long it takes, I'm willing to wait, for I won't regret it when I look into the eyes of my mate. So ladies, if you're looking for a Godly and wise man, wait on God. Gentlemen, if you're looking for a good virtuous woman, wait on God because in the midst of your waiting, God is preparing you for that special someone who will blow your mind and so you can be the man/woman that God has called you to be.

ı ı

Come

Come to me with all your matters and I'll give thee rest my child for I am meek and lowly, humble and holy, and my yolk is very mild. I'll give you peace, I'll keep you warm, I'll be your shelter in the time of the storm, I'll even protect you from all hurt and harm, come to me my child. You're the apple of my eye, my love for you I can't deny, I just want you to reply, come to me my child. My arms are open and stretched out wide, this love I have for you I can't keep inside, but why must you run and hide, come to me my child. Oh!, I notice you're walking towards me, I see that you hunger, you thirst, and life is getting worse and worse, but I'm the one you should've came to first, but still, come to me my child.

How to choose a mate

Lord, I will no longer seek you for just a mate, but I will also seek you for patience so that your perfect will can be done. Purify my emotions and cleanse my mind; help me to choose a mate according to Christian character and not according to my emotions for I know that "the heart (the emotions) is deceitful above all things and desperately wicked, who can know it?"

Who's First in Your Life?

He's my provider he protects me in the storm, when I'm cold, he keeps me warm. I can call on Jesus, he'll always be the same, he's the same from yesterday, he'll never change. So why not choose a friend like him? Why choose friends who would talk behind your back, lie on you, envy you and would even use you? Many times we forsake the one who loves us more than anyone, and that one is Jesus Christ. But when our friends or gone, we then decide to turn to Jesus, but why not turn to him now? For he's the one who loves you more than anyone ever could! Think about it!

Lazarus come forth

Lazarus was dead in his tomb, he began to stink and rot. Though the Jews did believe in miracles, they didn't believe that miracles could occur on the fourth day, only within three days of the individuals' death.   Jesus was informed of the death, but he hesitated, matter of fact, he arrived after the third day. When Jesus arrived, he was ready to demonstrate his power but one said "he stinketh" in other words, the third day had passed and the miracles could no longer happen. But Jesus turned his attention to the tomb where Lazarus rested and said, "Lazarus, come forth". All of a sudden, Lazarus walked out a whole new man. Jesus had to prove the Jews wrong, that's why he came on the fourth day. He wanted to show them that he could do the impossible. What's the situation in your life? Does it seem like nothing is going to happen? Does it seems like everything is just plain old dead? Well just when it seems impossible and you're at the lowest point of your life, the King of Kings and the Lord of Lords will step in and speak your deliverance to life!

I'm Blessed

I'm blessed coming in,
I'm blessed going out.
I'm blessed in the rain,
I'm blessed in a drought.

I'm blessed when I'm up,
blessed when I'm down,
blessed when I smile,
and blessed when I frown.

Blessed when I'm hungry,
blessed when I am filled
blessed when I'm sick,
and blessed when I'm healed.

Blessed when I'm sleep,
blessed when I wake.
blessed when in God's will,
and forgiven when I make mistakes.
I am blessed!

The Finishing Touch

Two customers went to a restaurant and ordered a steak dinner. As time went by, one of the customers got so impatient that she yelled to the tip of her voice, "I've been waiting too dag on long; I want my steak and I want it now! hurry up you scoundrel!" Well, the cook gave it to her and when she got home she opened her box and to her surprise, there was the steak by itself. It was half done. She said "Oh no! I'm taking this mess back!", so she stormed out the house and headed back to the restaurant. In the meantime, the other customer's order came up and when she came home, she opened her box and noticed that her steak was tender and juicy and on the side were steamed potatoes, julienne carrots(cut into strips), and a nice garden salad. She was very satisfied. The other customer finally arrived and stormed in the restaurant and complained at the cook, "Hey, what's your problem? all that was in my box was a half done steak, I ordered a meal!" The Cook replied "You must-have forgotten how you rushed me, so I gave it to you. If you allowed me to finish your meal, and add the finishing touches, your meal would've been complete! your impatience is what made your meal incomplete!" Well saints, that's how it works, we get so impatient some times and don't allow God to finish his plan, that when we take matters in our own hands and do things on our own, we fall. Many times, we give up and fall out the path right before God is about to manifest his blessings in our lives. Many of us are so, so close to our blessings. We need to allow God to add the finishing touches because your blessing is all most finished, it's on the way!

What is love?

Love is sweet, love is kind,
love is more valuable than
the most expensive bottle of wine.

Love is faithful, it never slacks,
it even confuses your enemies when
they expect you to get them back.

Love will never leave you, it will never leave you alone,
it will stick closer than the brother
when you feel you are on your own.

Love should be primary,
it will always stay near,
for God is that perfect love
and it casts out all fear.

Men Arise!

There was a couple that got into a heated argument while driving to the store. The man was so hurt and angry at what the woman said to him. They finally arrived at the store and the man went in by himself crying. All throughout the store, the man cried and cried. He finally got into the line and as he stood, he noticed a man behind him staring directly at him. And the man, who was crying, asked "sir, why are women so disobedient?" The man behind him replied "young man, the reason why women are so disobedient is because man has failed to submit to God!" Men it's time for us to arise. God has called us to be leaders of our families and households. It's time for us to carry revival upon our shoulders. Mama and Grandma have been doing it for too long. The moment we start taking care of business and be the type of man that God wants us to be, our children will be more obedient, our wives will be more reverent towards their husbands as leaders. The reason why our children are so loose and disrespectful towards adults is because there are not many male figures in their lives to keep them in check and to spend quality time with them. Not saying that women can't get the job done, but a child takes heed to the voice of a man more than anyone. The parents that are in the children's lives are not instilling the fear of God in their children either. The reason why so many women have an "independent woman mentality" is because they're, uh, independent. When a man submits to God, that lifestyle will linger on the woman and she too, will become a more humble vessel and submissive to God. Not meaning that she is to be quiet and unassertive, but meek, ladylike, one who acknowledges her husband as a leader and the head of the household. Men, we can make a difference. Men, let us be good to our children and make them feel special and if you have not been in the lives of your children, get into their lives and make a difference for that is God's will and expectancy. Let us be good to our wives and treat them like queens. Make them feel like you would not know what you would do without them. Men arise!

When Will I Thank God?

When will I thank God?
When I'm out?
When I'm delivered?
When I'm set free?
When I'm loosed?
When I'm happy?
When I'm calm?
When I'm rich?
When I'm fed?

Yes, but also:

When I'm bound!
When I'm in!
When I'm stuck!
When I'm imprisoned!
When I'm in a tight position!
When I'm sad!
When I'm roused up!
When I'm poor!
When I'm hungry!
In everything I will give thanks, for that is God's will in Christ
Jesus concerning me!

A burden

I had a burden, a great humongous burden. I went to church to get the victory, I went to the altar to see if he would fix it and the Holy Ghost set me free. What ever you need from God when you go to church, he can give it to you. The bible says "where two or three are gathered together in my name, there am I in the midst." When we get together to worship the King of Kings and the Lord of Lords, that's when Jesus himself will give a special visitation and touch us in a special way. It is very vital to attend church on a regular basis because it's at church where we get a special touch that we can't get at home! The Bible also tells us to "forsake not the assembly." If you haven't been to church lately and not sure which one to go to, seek the Lord and he will guide you where to go!

Power

Lord demonstrate your power in a weak and wicked land.

We need your anointing and a touch from your hands.

Lord demonstrate your power in a cold and wicked world.

Your love is open to every man, woman, boy and girl.

Lord you say!

Lord! you say you love me
and you say you care,
but why when I call you
it seems like you're not there?

You say you'll stick closer than a brother,
you say you'll be there to the end,
but when I'm lonely and I'm crying,
I feel like I have no friend.

Because I am human,
this is the way I feel,
but because of a word called faith,
I know that you are real.

I know that you love me
and you've always been kind,
you may not come when I want you,
but you are surely, always on time.

What Nerve!

Lord, I know you're angry at me,
I know I haven't been what I should have been.
But Lord, I have enough audacity to ask
you to withhold your judgment from me.
I know that I'm forgiven because I confessed and repented of my
sins.
But I also realize that repercussions must follow my sins.
But again, I am bold and assertive enough to
ask you cast off your anger towards me.

Lord You're Everything!

Jehovah, I praise you, for all of
the things, that you do, wonderful
counselor, the mighty God, the
everlasting father, Jehovah, I
praise you! You are the prince of
peace, king of all, a keeper when
I'm about to fall. A rose to my
delight, a beautiful lily in my sight.
A sweet taste of honey to my tongue,
and salvation to everyone. A fluffy
cloud in the sky, a healing comfort
when I cry. Lord, you are everything,
you are the reason why I praise and sing!

Disobedience

Disobedience sat on the wall,
disobedience had a great fall,
all the money, all the friends,
couldn't put disobedience together
again. But Jesus can my friend.
He'll come along and mend all
the broken fragments together.
He'll dust you off, pick you up,
turn you around, and place your
feet on solid ground!

⦙⦙⦙⦙⦙⦙⦙⦙⦙⦙⦙⦙⦙⦙⦙⦙⦙⦙⦙

Let us Pass Over!

Jesus told his disciples, "let us pass over to the other side."
They went on the boat and as they were on, a raging storm came.
The disciples were afraid and Jesus was asleep.
They woke Jesus up and he quieted the storm, and then questioned their faith.
The funny thing about it was that Jesus told the disciples, "let us go over to the other
side." It was final that they were to
go over to the other side for Jesus said it. So when the storm raged,
the disciple should've held on to God's word. Saints, what promises
has God gave you? If he said it, that settles it and nothing can reverse it!
So when the storm rages in your life, and it seems like the promises aren't
going to come to pass, hold on to God's promises, there's not a storm or
a combination of storms that can interfere with God's promises.
Just like the song says, "God said it, I believe it, I'm gonna take him at
his word."

⚜ ⚜ ⚜ ⚜ ⚜ ⚜ ⚜ ⚜ ⚜ ⚜ ⚜ ⚜

Hold On!

Jesus took five loaves of bread and two fish a lifted his head to heaven and blessed it. He broke the food into pieces and fed 5,000 men, who possibly had their wives and children with them. So that's man, woman, and 2 children approximately; possibly equaling 20,000 people. As Jesus broke the bread and divided the fish, the food was miraculously multiplying in his hands so that all would be fed. After the people departed, Jesus gave the disciples twelve baskets and they filled them with fragments. Jesus performed a miracle for the people and the disciples. Jesus went to a mountain to pray. The disciples went on a ship and as time went by the wind became very violent. The disciples were very afraid. When Jesus saw what was going on, from the land he was standing on, he appeared before them. When it was all over, they made it to dry land safely. The problem with the disciples was that they didn't consider the miracle Jesus had performed for them previously. The bible says, "their hearts were hardened." If they considered the miracle, they would've said to themselves that the God that performed the previous miracle was the same God that would've took them through the storm. Saints, when God performs a miracle in your life, hold on to the miracle so that when the storm rages in your life, you can consider them and be encouraged and know that if God performed miraculous blessings in the past, he will do the same in the present. In Psalms 77, Asaph said, "I considered the times of old." In other words, when he was going through hardships, he considered the good things God did in his life and he stayed encouraged. Saints, look back!

Gospel Stage Plays!

I love gospel stage plays, but as much as I love them, there is one main thing that disturbs me and that is how when many relationships turn sour, one chooses to get revenge in an unforgiving manner. Many people give such an act a standing ovation and cheer it on and unfortunately, many are church goers who claims to believe in a certain book called the Bible which tells us to FORGIVE! Are we to follow after Christ's example and forgive those that wrong us? When one cheats on the other, whether they divorce or stay with one another, they are to forgive nonetheless. When we're at a stage play and unforgiveness is involved, we are not to stand and cheer it on because unforgiveness is SIN!

Forgive!

Forgive your neighbors when they treat
wrong, turn the other way and sing a happy song.

Forgive your neighbors when they persecute
and hurt you, Give it over to Jesus and he'll see
you through.

Forgive your neighbors when they sing
to you a negative tune,
Jesus will heal your scars and care for your wounds!

More Than Anything!

Give me Jesus, I want him more than anything.
I want him more than money, silver, gold and diamond
rings. I want him more than anything.

Homes, fancy cars, and hotels with 5 stars. I
want him more than anything. Reputation, respect,
fame, friends, status and even a good name. I want him more than
anything.

Jesus comes first, he's always on top, my praise, worship,
reverence and adoration will never stop. I want him more than
anything.

⁖⁖⁖⁖⁖⁖⁖⁖⁖⁖⁖⁖⁖⁖⁖⁖⁖⁖

Victory!

In the days that kings and queens reigned, kings wore what you call trains.
Trains were long, cape-like garments that kings wore on their backs.
The length of the train symbolized the number of victories won in battle.
So, if one wanted to challenge a king with an extremely long train, the challenger should think twice for he was destined to lose. Isaiah the prophet went in the temple and saw the Lord sitting on the throne and his train filled the temple. Now the temple was humongus and for a train to fill it meant that it was ridiculously long! Therefore, our Lord is ridiculously victorious! We have the victory through our Lord Jesus Christ. This is probably why the Bible tells us that we are more than conquerors because God's train is more than enough for us to overcome any battle. So saints, the next time you are struggling with a situation, think of the Lords train. Satan knows that God dwells in you, and he knows that the God in you has a lengthy train, so he'll think twice before he challenges you, because Satan knows he's a loser!

What's on the Inside?

A woman asked God, "God, why won't you respond to my heart anymore?" God replied, because it's too crowded in there, your job is in there, I see your boyfriend, and oh!, that nice fancy car of yours I see as well, see my child, you have put all those things before me and left me out, the one who supplied you with those things (except that boyfriend of yours, I'm not sure about him). The woman realized what she had done and fell on her knees and repented and redirected her life back to God, and she also let go of that unsaved man of her's as well! See, we should never seek those things that collects dust and can even die, but the one who can supply them, and that one is Jesus. He will add these things to us if we seek him and his righteousness first! The bible tells us if we draw nigh to God, he will draw nigh to us. So if it seems like God has not responded to you in a while, ask yourself, "have I been seeking his face and communicating with him in prayer and devotion?" If the answer is NO, that's why. If the answer is YES, the trying of your faith will work patience. Who/what's first in your life?

Where To Go

There was once an old lady who was suffering from a tooth ache. She decided to go to the grocery store to get it fixed. She went to customer service and explained her situation and they told her that they couldn't help her. She went to the beauty salon and they too, turned her down. After visiting a restaurant, a club and even a theme park, she finally went to the dentist. She told the dentist about her tooth ache and he said, "well, you came to the right place." Well saints, that tells us that we need to go to the right source. When we commit a sin, we should repent unto God, the right source. Many times, we find ourselves confessing our faults to our friends first instead of God. God should be the first and in some cases, the only one we should confess our sins to for he is the only one that can wash away our sins! Also, if need be, we should never hesitate to talk to our pastor, for he/she watches for our souls. Therefore, he/she will encourage us to repent.

I Have a Feeling

I have a feeling that everything's going to be alright.
Not only is there weeping, but there is also joy in the night.
Hold up the fight, be a light, rise to new heights,
hold to God's hand tight and when it's all over,
it'll be a gracious sight.

The Bible tells us that "weeping may endure for a night,
but joy cometh in the morning." One day, the Lord told me
that we, the people of God, can have joy in the night time as well.

Had Your Daily Fruit?

Fruit contains the essential vitamins and nutrients needed for the body. Fruits such as oranges that contains vitamin C (ascorbic acid). Or bananas that contain potassium, etc. Natural fruit is good for the human body but profits nothing for the spirit. That's why the fruits of the spirit, spoken in the Bible (Galatians chapter 5), is very important for our spiritual being. The fruits of the spirit contains 9 essentials, and those are love, joy, peace, longsuffering, gentleness, goodness, faith, meekness, and temperance. These can't be eaten, but practiced! Practicing these everyday will promote a Godly lifestyle!

What is a Man of God?
Dedicated to Jason Bryant

A man flaunt his muscles and struts his stuff, but a man of God
stands on his two feet when times get rough.

A man will leave his family when he feels that he can't cope, but a
man of
God will lift his eyes unto the hills when he feels there's no hope.

A man will find the easy way out due to hard ships and fear, but a
man of God will stay
in the heat of the battle because God said "the buck stops here."

Jason Bryant is not a real man according to his physic or his bod,
but Jason is a real man because he fears and reverences God!

What is a Woman of God
Dedicated to Shante Bryant

A woman flaunts, sashes and switches with her hips,
but a woman of God walks accordingly with praises from her lips.

A woman is independent, and can take care of herself, but a
woman of God looks
unto the hills from which cometh her help.

A woman is talented, skillful and has that special touch, but a
woman of God
is fearfully and wondrously made and most definitely virtuous.

Shante Bryant is that woman of God that Jason has been longing
for, Shante didn't come
from just any where, but she came strictly from the Lord!

The Bitterness of the Word

When one entered the holy place of the tabernacle, they would notice a table with some flat bread. When it was eaten, the consumer would notice that the bread was bitter. That's because the bread was sprinkled with bitter herbs. The bread, along with many other things, was a figure of what was to come and that figure was Jesus Christ. Now Jesus is the bread of life and the bread on the table represents the word of God. The bitter herbs represents bitterness of Gods word, meaning that the word of God may be bitter or offensive, but good for our spiritual being. Now saints, y'all know what I'm talking about! Many times when the word comes across, it doesn't always stick well, but it's good for our spiritual being. Next time your pastor preach and it offends you, just know that you just took a big bite of bread with a mouth full of herbs!

The Blood

B-l-o-o-d was the blood of Jesus Christ that was shed for me.

He shed his blood on Calvary, that you and I may be set free.

Because of this, I have victory and power to tread on the head of the enemy.

I am free, yes I am, all because of the blood of a little lamb.

The Light in Darkness

There was a black out in a building and everyone was asked to evacuate it. Many people were feeling on the walls and crawling on the ground just to find their way out. There was only one person who had a flash light in the building and when the people, who were in darkness, saw the light, they drew themselves to that person and he led them out the building. He went back to lead other people out. Well, we are the light of the world. We live in a world of darkness. When the world sees our light, they will come and dwell among us so we, with the help of Jesus, can lead them out of darkness. We are to guide them out by preaching the gospel and living the life. It's amazing how God has "called us out of darkness and into his marvelous light." "We are the lights of the world, a city on a hill that can not be hid." In other words everyone can see it!

Lord, Work on Me

Though I'm in the fire and am being tried,
Jesus is standing right by my side.
He's my source and he's my guide.
His love for me he's never denied.
Sometimes I want to run and hide,
due to discouragement, stubbornness and pride.
Lord please work on my insides,
so I may be able to say "to myself, I have died."
(In other words, I have died out to the flesh
for Paul said, "I die daily")

Joke
The Lord's Miracle

There was a man who was drinking under the influence of alcohol. He was speeding and was stopped by a police officer. The officer asked him was he drinking and the man told him no. The officer noticed a bottle in the back of his car and asked the driver about it. The driver replied "that's nothing but water." The officer took the bottle and smelled it. The officer told the man to step out of the car because that bottle contained pure vodka. The driver replied, "oh my, the Lord dun done it again, he dun turned water into wine." LOL!

Looking From the Outside In

A man was walking down the street and suddenly, he heard a great commotion coming from a particular house. He walked to the house and looked through the family's window. He noticed that the man of the house was jumping up and down! Looking crazy. The man, looking through the window from outside, walked away and said "that's ill-mannered and uncouth people for ya!" As time went by, the man went to a music entertainment restaurant and to his surprise, he saw that crazy family up on the stage singing a song. They sung so beautifully that everyone, including him, gave the family a standing ovation. The man went to the man of the family after the performance, and complimented him and his family for the awesome performance. But the man had to ask him "what was your problem that day, jumping all over the place, are you crazy?" The man replied "how would you react if a big time record company called you up and offered you a big record deal?" The man replied "well I didn't know, it looked so bizarre"; the man, of the family, said "that's because you were looking from the outside in." Sounds familiar? Saints, we live in a world where people are so self-righteous and our world is so full of hypocrisy, contradiction and paradox. People are looking from the outside in, where they see something and quickly make a conclusion, instead of walking in and finding out what's going on, or at least broadening their minds and giving the benefit of the doubt. It probably would've been inappropriate for the man to knock on the door and ask what was going on, but he should've at least walked away with more than one possible conclusion without yielding to neither one until the truth was revealed! Looks may be deceiving folks!

Patience is the Way

There was once a young man who saw a young lady at church and boy, was she fine! The young man said "I would love to talk to her, but I'm going to wait." As weeks went by, the young man saw the young lady out with some friends and by the young man's surprise, the young lady and her friends were cursing up a storm and they were also dressed provocatively. The young lady didn't exhilarate Christian virtues and character. The young man said to himself, "I'm so glad I waited because patience was the weapon that caused deception to reveal itself!" What may look good on the outside isn't good on the inside! It's just like grilling chicken for only one minute. It may look good and done on the outside, but the inside is raw and full of salmonella (food borne illness deriving from uncooked poultry) on the inside! Once again, looks can be deceiving.

· ｜ · ｜ · ｜ · ｜ · ｜ · ｜ · ｜ · ｜ · ｜ · ｜ · ｜ · ｜ · ｜ · ｜ · ｜ ·

Racism

Lord, why is there so much racism in the world? It's the epitome of stupidity! It's a shame that people don't like others on the basis of skin color. There are various shades of dust that exist and each match the different shades of people's skin color in the world. The word of God says that Adam was formed from dust and he shall return as dust. We are all dust and this is nothing but a dust war!

ı ı

Godly Ordination

There was a woman who had several bad experiences with men of her own race. She decided to date men of other races and when a man of her own race approached her, she bluntly told them, "I no longer date men of my own race!" There's a major problem this day where people have developed a habit of putting all of one group of people in a box instead of individualizing them. It hurts me deeply to hear some one speak negative about a whole group of people, when only a handful of the group wronged them. That's not fair to the other 99%. We need to stop thinking that other races are better because in God's eyes "all have sinned and fell short of the glory of God." It's not a race issue, it's a God's will issue. We should not desire a mate on basis of past experiences or skin color, but on the person's relationship with God. If a man loves God, he will love his woman as Christ loves the church. It also depends on God's will. The reason why many relationships don't work out is not because of skin color, but it wasn't God oriented. So ladies and gentlemen, if you think that turning to other races will make things better, it wont because any relationship that's not God-oriented will not work out! I am not against interracial relationships nor do I have a problem with racial preference. I am for it all the way; I think it's a beautiful thing. I just have a problem when people put a whole group of people in a box due to what less than 1% of the group did. If you wait on the Lord for the right mate, he will send you the man/woman that you've been longing for regardless of race or past experiences!

Look to Jesus

Trials here, trials there,
trials are everywhere,
but Jesus Christ, he really cares!

He's not a God that will
just throw you away;
he'll stick closer than a brother,
all night and all day!

People can disappoint you
and make you want to leave,
but Jesus Christ
can touch your heart
and make you want to cleave!

So always look to Jesus,
whether people are near or far;
he desires to hear your problems,
no matter where you are!

So cast all your cares upon him,
for he careth for his flock;
he will freely open his entrance,
his doors will never lock!

This poem came semi-finalist place in he International Open Poetry Contest

Though

Though I lose my job, I'm working for Jesus
Though my finances get low, I'm rich in spirit
Though I'm stressed, I'm blessed
Though my lights are turned off, I'm the light of the world
Though my life feels like dead weeds, I'm a tree planted by the
waters
Though I hunger, I'm filled
Though Satan is on my trail, Jesus is in my heart
Regardless of the negative, the positive will over rule!

Wonderful!

Wonderful Jesus, bright morning star
you're the lily of the valley,
that's what you are. Wonderful
savior, you are so true, wonderful
Jesus, how I love you!

Joke

There was an old man who vowed to himself that he would ride a go cart before he die and go to heaven. So his daughter took him to a go-cart park. The operator told him in order for the go-cart to accelerate, he must say "thank you Jesus", in order for it to stop, he must say, "oh Lord!" So the old man said "thank you Jesus", and the cart accelerated. After a while, the old man wanted to go faster, so he said "thank you Jesus", and the cart went even faster. He loved it, so he said "thank you Jesus, thank you Jesus, heh! heh!", and the cart went super fast. The old man began to panic and tried to stop it. So he said "thank you Jesus", but the cart went even faster. He actually forgot how to stop it, so he kept saying, "thank you Jesus, thank you Jesus, thank you Jesus", and the cart kept going faster, and faster, and faster. The old man knew it was over for him, he even said "Lord I don't deserve this!" He was nearing a cliff and right before the cart rolled off, he remembered how to stop it and said "oh Lord!" and the cart stopped immediately at the tip of the cliff. The old man was so grateful and overjoyed that he leaned back in the cart and said "Whew! thank you Jesus". LOL!

Printed in the United States
46524LVS00002B/7-9